To a very special person
with all my love
Julie
xxx

THE COUNTRYSIDE

THE COUNTRYSIDE

An Illustrated Treasury

Compiled by Michelle Lovric

COURAGE
BOOKS

an imprint of
RUNNING PRESS
Philadelphia • London

The author gratefully acknowledges the permission of the following
to reproduce copyrighted material in this book:

P. 8: From "Fern Hill" by Dylan Thomas, from *The Poems*, published
in the U.S.A. by New Directions, Inc., and in the U.K. by J. M.
Dent & Co. Ltd. Copyright © The Trustees for the copyright of the
late Dylan Thomas. By permission of David Higham Associates and
New Directions, Inc.

P. 24: From "Respite," from *Straight Lines* by William Neill, published by Blackstaff Press, Belfast. Copyright © 1992 William Neill.

P. 30: "From the Lanes," from *New Pastorals* by Robert Etty, published by Crabflower Pamphlets. Copyright © 1992 Robert Etty.

P. 34: From a poem by Claudian, from *More Latin Lyrics*, translated
by Helen Waddell and edited by Dame Felicitas Corrigan,
published by Victor Gollancz Ltd., London. Copyright © 1976
Stanbrook Abbey.

P. 42: From *Song of Solomon* by Toni Morrison, published in the
U.S.A. and Canada by Alfred A. Knopf, and in the U.K. by Chatto
& Windus. Copyright © 1977 Toni Morrison. By permission of
Chatto & Windus and International Creative Management, Inc.

Introduction

The town is the face, and the country is the soul of the world, it is said. Town and country often are seen in opposition: sophistication pitted against simplicity, artifice against nature, restless change against tranquility.

From the city, the countryside is seen as a heartland that both arouses and soothes the senses and the soul. In the country, we feel at peace and yet somehow more aware. The constant cycle of growth and renewal is there, undiluted, before us. Indeed, no matter how far we live from the country, we carry its rhythms in our blood and recognize its influence in our hearts and minds.

The countryside—in imagination as in reality—has been reinvented by humankind. Our tools have shaped it and our culture has overlaid it with symbolic meanings. Associated with it are all the virtues and pleasures of a wholesome life: natural beauty, quiet peace, honest toil. "Back to Nature!" we cry, meaning back to simplicity, truth, and goodness, as well as greenness.

This book explores in words and images the way we respond to the countryside: what we ask of it, how we celebrate it, and how it answers us with its blessings.

MAY THE COUNTRYSIDE AND

THE GLIDING VALLEY STREAMS

CONTENT ME.

LOST TO FAME, LET ME LOVE RIVER

AND WOODLAND.

Virgil [Publius Vergilius Maro] (70–19 B.C.)
Roman poet

We were dreamers, dreaming greatly,
  in the men-stifled town;
We yearned beyond the sky-line. . . .

RUDYARD KIPLING (1865–1936)
ENGLISH WRITER

AND I WAS GREEN AND CAREFREE, FAMOUS AMONG THE BARNS

ABOUT THE HAPPY YARD AND SINGING AS THE FARM WAS HOME,

IN THE SUN THAT IS YOUNG ONCE ONLY,

TIME LET ME PLAY AND BE

GOLDEN IN THE MERCY OF HIS MEANS,

AND GREEN AND GOLDEN I WAS HUNTSMAN AND HERDSMAN, THE CALVES

SANG TO MY HORN, THE FOXES ON THE HILL BARKED CLEAR AND COLD,

AND THE SABBATH RANG SLOWLY

IN THE PEBBLES OF THE HOLY STREAMS.

Dylan Thomas (1914–1953)
Welsh poet

To one who has been long in city pent,

'Tis very sweet to look into the fair

And open face of heaven.

JOHN KEATS (1795–1821)
ENGLISH POET

*Just as sunlight exceeds starlight,
so the country, for true and
lasting beauty, exceeds the city.*

DR. E. DAVIES
19TH-CENTURY ENGLISH WRITER

With the wasp at the innermost heart of a peach,

On a sunny wall out of tip-toe reach,

With the trout in the darkest summer pool,

With the fern-seed clinging behind its cool

Smooth frond, in the chink of an aged tree,

In the woodbine's horn with the drunken bee,

With the mouse in the nest in the furrow old,

With the chrysalis wrapt in its gauzy fold;

With things that are hidden, and safe, and bold,

With things that are timid, and shy, and free,

Wishing to be

Dora Greenwell (1821–1882)
English poet and writer

THE HOME OF MY CHILDHOOD, ETERNAL AND GREEN, APPEARS BEFORE MY INWARD EYE. . . . NO MATTER WHERE I AM, I SEEK UNCONSCIOUSLY FOR RESEMBLANCES TO THAT BELOVED SPOT.

Alison Uttley (1884–1976)
English writer

Within me cornfields rustle. . . .

VACHEL LINDSAY (1879–1931)
AMERICAN POET

*Knowest thou the land where
the lemon-trees bloom?
In the dark foliage the golden
oranges gleam,
A soft wind blows from the
blue heavens,
The myrtle is still and the laurel
stands high.*

JOHANN VON GOETHE (1749–1832)
GERMAN POET

Look! under that broad beech-tree I sat down, when I was last this way a-fishing; and the birds in the adjoining grove seemed to have a friendly contention with an echo, whose dead voice seemed to live in a hollow tree near to the brow of that primrose hill. There I sat viewing the silver streams glide silently towards their center, the tempestuous sea.

Izaak Walton (1593–1683)
English writer

I remember, I remember,
The fir-trees dark and high. . . .

THOMAS HOOD (1799–1845)
ENGLISH POET

THERE IS NOTHING HALF SO GREEN THAT I KNOW ANYWHERE, AS THE GRASS OF THAT CHURCHYARD; NOTHING HALF SO SHADY AS ITS TREES; NOTHING HALF SO QUIET AS ITS TOMBSTONES. THE SHEEP ARE FEEDING THERE, WHEN I KNEEL UP, EARLY IN THE MORNING, IN MY LITTLE BED IN A CLOSET WITHIN MY MOTHER'S ROOM, TO LOOK OUT AT IT; AND I SEE THE RED LIGHT SHINING ON THE SUN-DIAL, AND THINK WITHIN MYSELF, "IS THE SUN-DIAL GLAD, I WONDER, THAT IT CAN TELL THE TIME AGAIN?"

Charles Dickens (1812–1870)
English writer

nineteen

$\mathcal{H}$OW GLORIOUSLY BEAUTIFUL THE COUNTRY WAS! IT WAS SUMMER TIME; THE CORN WAS YELLOW, THE OATS WERE GREEN, THE HAY WAS STACKED UP IN THE FRAGRANT MEADOWS; THE STORK WALKED PROUDLY ABOUT ON HIS LONG RED LEGS, TALKING EGYPTIAN TO HIMSELF, THE LANGUAGE HE HAD LEARNED FROM HIS MOTHER. GREAT WOODS STOOD ROUND THE CORN-FIELDS AND MEADOW LANDS; AND HIDDEN IN THE WOODS WERE STILL, DEEP LAKES.

Hans Christian Andersen (1805–1875)
Danish writer

IN THE COUNTRY IT IS AS IF EVERY TREE SAID TO ME "HOLY! HOLY!" WHO CAN EVER EXPRESS THE ECSTASY OF THE WOODS?

IF ALL ELSE FAILS, THERE REMAINS THE COUNTRY, EVEN IN WINTER.

Ludwig van Beethoven (1770–1827)
German composer

There is pleasure in the pathless woods,
There is rapture on the lonely shore
There is society, where none intrudes,
By the deep Sea, and Music in its roar:
I love not Man the less, but Nature more.

GEORGE GORDON, LORD BYRON (1788–1824)
ENGLISH POET

Men commute amazing distances in order to wake up to the sound of bird chatter.

ANNE SCOTT-JAMES, B. 1913
ENGLISH JOURNALIST AND WRITER

NO CONVERSATION HERE BUT THE WIND'S VOICE,

THE RUSTLE OF TREES, BIRD SONG AND SECRET CALLS

IN DARK OR MOONLIGHT. FROST CRISP OVER GRASS,

RAIN ON THE CHEEK. AFTER THE RUMBLING CITY

THIS PEACE ASSAILS THE EAR.

TIME HERE FOR SUNDRY OLD PHILOSOPHIES

THAT HANG FROM BOUGHS OR WHISPER AMONG LEAVES.

William Neill, b. 1922
Scottish poet

I never enter this delicious retirement
but my spirits are revived, and a sweet
complacency diffuses itself over my
whole mind.

SIR RICHARD STEELE (1672–1729)
IRISH POET AND WRITER

The damasked meadows and the pebbly streams

Sweeten and make soft your dreams:

The purling springs, groves, birds and well-weaved bowers,

With fields enamellèd with flowers,

Present their shapes, while fantasy discloses

Millions of lilies mixed with roses.

ROBERT HERRICK (1591–1674)
ENGLISH POET

EVERYTHING IS QUIET. LISTEN TO THE BEES! WHAT MEADOWS GO DOWN THERE TO THE PLAIN! WHAT RICH TREES ARE ABOUT US,—ELMS, OAKS, AND BEECHES; NOT RICH IN FRUIT, BUT RICH IN VERDURE AND LEAVES, AND FOOD FOR POETRY.

Leigh Hunt (1784–1859)
English poet and writer

The landscape . . . speaks gravely of eternity.

RAINER MARIA RILKE (1875–1926)
CZECH-BORN GERMAN POET

*I*T IS A GOOD THING TO LIVE IN THE COUNTRY—TO ESCAPE FROM THE PRISON WALLS OF THE METROPOLIS—THE GREAT BRICKERY WE CALL "THE CITY"—AND TO LIVE AMID BLOSSOMS AND LEAVES, IN SHADOW AND SUNSHINE, IN MOONLIGHT AND STARLIGHT, IN RAIN, MIST, DEW, HOARFROST, AND DROUGHT, OUT IN THE OPEN CAMPAIGN, AND UNDER THE BLUE DOME THAT IS BOUNDED BY THE HORIZON ONLY. IT IS A GOOD THING TO HAVE A WELL WITH DRIPPING BUCKETS, A PORCH WITH HONEY BUDS AND SWEET BELLS, A HIVE EMBROIDERED WITH NIMBLE BEES, A SUNDIAL MOSSED OVER, IVY UP TO THE EAVES, CURTAINS OF DIMITY, A TUMBLER OF FRESH FLOWERS IN YOUR BEDROOM, A ROOSTER ON THE ROOF, AND A DOG UNDER THE PIAZZA.

Frederick S. Cozzens (1818–1869)
American writer

The country habit has me by the heart.....

GAZING ACROSS THE TABLECLOTH, YOU REMINISCED.

YOUR VOICE SOUNDED AS DISTANT AS THE YEARS,

THE TRAMS AND CORN EXCHANGE, BIKE RIDES FOR VIOLETS

AND CELANDINES THAT YOU BASKETED HOME AND PRESSED.

HEAT LAY LIKE AN EIDERDOWN. GNATS DOTTED THE SKY.

AND AS YOU SPOKE I SQUEEZED ONTO MY TONGUE

THE TANG OF THE FRUIT OUR THORNED FINGERS PICKED

FOR YOU TO BAKE A RHUBARB AND RASPBERRY PIE.

Robert Etty
20th-century British teacher and poet

It is a vulgar error to suppose that you have tasted huckleberries who never plucked them.

HENRY DAVID THOREAU (1817–1862)
AMERICAN WRITER

What happiness to sit on this tufty knoll, and fill my basket with the blossoms! What a renewal of heart and mind! To inhabit such a scene of peace and sweetness is again to be fearless, gay, and gentle as a child. Then it is that thought becomes poetry. . . .

Mary Russell Mitford (1787–1855)
English playwright and writer

BREATHLESS, WE FLUNG US
ON THE WINDY HILL,
LAUGHED IN THE SUN, AND KISSED
THE LOVELY GRASS.

Rupert Brooke (1887–1915)
English poet

Cultivate simplicity, or rather, I should say, banish elaborateness; for simplicity springs spontaneous from the heart, and carries into daylight on its own buds of genuine, sweet, and clear flowers of expression.

Charles Lamb (1775–1834)
English writer

HOW BLESSED IS HE, WHO

    LEADS A COUNTRY LIFE,

UNVEX'D WITH ANXIOUS CARES,

    AND VOID OF STRIFE!

WHO STUDYING PEACE,

    AND SHUNNING CIVIL RAGE,

ENJOY'D HIS YOUTH AND

    NOW ENJOYS HIS AGE:

ALL WHO DESERVE HIS LOVE,

    HE MAKES HIS OWN;

AND, TO BE LOV'D HIMSELF,

    NEEDS ONLY TO BE KNOWN.

John Dryden (1631–1700)
English poet

This man has lived his life
in his own fields
The house that saw him
as a little lad
Sees him as an old man. . . .
Let you go gadding,
gape at farthest Spain:
You'll have seen life; but this
old man has lived.

CLAUDIAN (370–405)
ROMAN POET
TRANSLATED BY HELEN WADDELL

To those far from the city and steeped in all that varies and does not die, to them alone does each day bring with it the certainty of change, of labor which strives toward perfection, of plant and animal life which proclaims, "I am resplendent still. Already I am become active. . . ."

Colette [Sidonie-Gabrielle] (1873–1954)
French writer

The common growth of Mother Earth

Suffices me—her tears, her mirth. . . .

William Wordsworth (1770–1850)
English poet

*T*he big doors of the country barn stand open and ready,

The dried grass of the harvest-time loads the slow-drawn wagon,

The clear light plays on the brown gray and green intertinged,

The armfuls are pack'd to the sagging mow.

I am here, I help, I came stretch'd atop of the load,

I felt its soft jolts, one leg reclined on the other,

I jump from the cross-beams and seize the clover and timothy,

And roll head over heels and tangle my hair full of wisps.

WALT WHITMAN (1819–1892)
AMERICAN POET

TOUCH THE EARTH, LOVE THE EARTH, HONOR THE EARTH.

Henry Beston (1888–1968)
American writer

Earth is dearer than gold.

ESTONIAN PROVERB

forty

$\mathcal{B}$UT THE LAND—IT IS ONE THING THAT WILL STILL BE THERE WHEN I COME BACK—LAND IS ALWAYS THERE.

Pearl S. Buck (1892–1973)
American writer and humanitarian

"You see?" the farm said to them. "See? See what you can do? Never mind you can't tell one letter from another, never mind you born a slave, never mind you lose your name, never mind your daddy dead, never mind nothing. Here, this here, is what a man can do if he puts his mind to it, and his back in it."

TONI MORRISON, B. 1931
AMERICAN WRITER

THERE IS LIFE IN THE GROUND: IT GOES
UP INTO THE SEEDS; AND IT ALSO,
WHEN IT IS STIRRED UP, GOES INTO
THE MAN WHO STIRS IT.

Charles Dudley Warner (1829–1900)
American writer

Earth is here so kind, that just tickle her with a hoe and she laughs with a harvest.

DOUGLAS JERROLD (1803–1857)
ENGLISH WRITER

TO PLOW IS TO PRAY—TO PLANT IS TO
PROPHESY, AND THE HARVEST
ANSWERS AND FULFILLS.

Robert Green Ingersoll (1833–1899)
American lawyer and writer

No occupation is so delightful to me as the culture of the earth.

THOMAS JEFFERSON (1743–1826)
THIRD PRESIDENT OF THE UNITED STATES

*I*N THE FURROWED LAND

THE TOILSOME AND PATIENT OXEN STAND;

LIFTING THE YOKE-ENCUMBERED HEAD,

WITH THEIR DILATED NOSTRILS SPREAD,

THEY SILENTLY INHALE

THE CLOVER-SCENTED GALE,

AND THE VAPOURS THAT ARISE

FROM THE WELL-WATERED AND SMOKING SOIL.

Henry Wadsworth Longfellow (1807–1882)
American poet

For who loves me must have a touch of earth.

ALFRED, LORD TENNYSON (1809–1892)
ENGLISH POET

Now fades the glimmering
 landscape on the sight,
And all the air a solemn
 stillness holds,
Save where the beetle wheels
 his droning flight,
And drowsy tinklings lull the
 distant folds.

THOMAS GRAY (1716–1771)
ENGLISH POET

There rolls the deep where grew the tree.

O earth, what changes hast thou seen!

There where the long street roars, hath been

The stillness of the central sea.

The hills are shadows, and they flow

From form to form, and nothing stands;

They melt like mist, the solid lands,

Like clouds they shape themselves and go.

But in my spirit will I dwell,

And dream my dream, and hold it true;

For though my lips may breathe adieu,

I cannot think the thing farewell.

Alfred, Lord Tennyson (1809–1892)
English poet

ILLUSTRATION ACKNOWLEDGMENTS

COVER: *A Riverside Cottage in Summer*, T. Noelsmith (Fine Lines (Fine Art), Shipston-on-Stour, Warks)

TITLE PAGE [detail]: *Autumn in the North*, Vernon Ward

p. 7: *The River Dove*, Rex Preston (Granby Gallery, Bakewell)

p. 9: *Buttermere—The Picnic*, Rex Preston (Granby Gallery, Bakewell)

p. 10 [detail]: *Woodland Glory*, Vernon Ward

p. 12: *A Riverside Cottage in Summer*, T. Noelsmith (Fine Lines (Fine Art), Shipston-on-Stour, Warks)

p. 15: *Children Resting*, John Anthony Puller

p. 16: *Anglers All*, John Haskins (Daryl Davies (British Fine Art), Ringwood, Hampshire)

p. 19 [detail]: *Salisbury Cathedral*, James Fletcher-Watson

p. 20: *Corn Field on the Isle of Wight*, Richard Burchett (Victoria & Albert Museum, London, and Bridgeman Art Library, London)

p. 22 [detail]: *Old Harry Rocks*, Vernon Ward

p. 25 [detail]: *Blackbird, Nest & Wild Roses*, Gillean Whitaker

p. 27: *Daisies & Poppies, Norfolk*, Maurice Read

p. 29: *Sunflowers*, Stephen Oliver (Image by Design)

p. 31: *The Cabbage Patch*, Alfred Augustus Glendening, Sr. (Fine Art Photographic Library Limited)

p. 32 [detail]: *Vale of Pewsey, Wiltshire*, Ronald Maddox PRI Hon.RWS FCSD (© Ronald Maddox)

p. 35 [detail]: *Spring*, John Corcoran

p. 37 [detail]: *The Hen Coop*, Miles Birkett Foster (Worthing Museum & Art Gallery)

p. 39: *Haymaking Near Meriden*, Robert J. Hammond (Fine Art Photographic Library Limited)

p. 40: *Near Devil's Dyke, Brighton*, John Constable

p. 42–43: *Easterly Winds*, Vernon Ward

p. 45 [detail]: *Oxen at Chantilly*, Sir Alfred Munnings (© Sir Alfred Munnings Art Museum, Dedham, Essex)

p. 46–47: *Moonlight Over Scottish Loch*, Geoffrey Stone